COROT

SPRING ART BOOKS

COROT

BY KEITH ROBERTS

SPRING BOOKS • LONDON

ACKNOWLEDGMENTS

The paintings in this volume are reproduced by kind permission of the following collections and galleries to which they belong: Albright-Knox Art Gallery, Buffalo, N.Y. (Plate 10); Ashmolean Museum, Oxford (Plates 2, 34); Brooklyn Museum, New York (Plate 47); Chicago Art Institute, Mr and Mrs Martin A. Ryerson Collection (Plate 14); Glasgow Art Gallery (Plate 48); Kröller-Müller Museum, Otterlo (Plate 12); Kunsthaus, Zürich (Plate 8); Metropolitan Museum of Art, Rogers Fund 1938 (Plate 17); Musée du Louvre, Paris, Personnaz Bequest, 1935 (Plate 22); Musée du Louvre, Paris (Plates 1, 3, 4, 5, 11, 16, 18, 21, 23, 30, 32, 35, 37, 39, 40, 41, 42; 43, 44, 45, 49, 51); Musée des Beaux-Arts, Reims (Plates 19, 46); Musée des Beaux-Arts, Strasbourg (Plate 26); Musée du Petit-Palais, Paris (Plate 25); Musée de Quimper (Plate 24); Musée de Saint-Lô (Plate 28); Museum of Fine Arts, Boston (Plates 9, 29); Museum of Fine Arts, Springfield (Plate 27); the National Gallery of Canada, Ottawa (Plate 6); the Trustees of the National Gallery, London (Plates 7, 33, 50); the National Gallery of Victoria, Melbourne, Felton Bequest (Plate 15); National Gallery of Art, Washington, D.C., Chester Dale Collection (Plates 13, 20); the Trustees of the Wallace Collection, London (Plate 38); Yale University Art Gallery, Bequest of Stephen Carlton Clark (Plate 31). The black and white photographs in this volume are reproduced by kind permission of: the Ashmolean Museum, Oxford (Figure 5); the Trustees of the British Museum, London (Figure 3); Musée Cantini, Marseilles (Figure 7); Musée des Arts Decoratifs, Paris (Figure 2); Musée du Louvre, Paris (Figure 1); Museum Boymans-van Beuningen, Rotterdam (Figure 6); Palais des Beaux-Arts, Lille (Figure 4). The frontispiece is reproduced by courtesy of the Gernsheim Collection, London.

The following photographs were supplied by Michael Holford, London (Plates 5, 16, 25, 28, 33, 34, 36, 38, 50); Jacqueline Hyde, Paris (Plates 1, 3, 4, 7, 11, 18, 21, 22, 23, 30, 32, 35, 37, 39, 40, 41, 42, 43, 44, 45, 49, 51 and Figure 1); Photographie Giraudon, Paris (Plate 46); Photographie Rigoir (Figure 7).

Published by
SPRING BOOKS
Westbook House • Fulham Broadway • London
© Paul Hamlyn Ltd 1965
Printed in Czechoslovakia by Svoboda, Prague
T 1566

CONTENTS

THE BLACK AND WHITE ILLUSTRATIONS

INTRODUCTION

On the 10th of February, 1875, the curé of Coubron, a small village where Corot had built himself a studio two years before, came to Paris to administer the last sacraments to the dying painter. "What a man!" he was moved to exclaim as he left. "I have never seen anyone like him." *Quel homme! Je n'ai jamais vu son pareil.* The curé had been deeply impressed, as were all those who knew the artist in old age, by the fineness of Corot's character. By the 1860s he had become the world's foremost landscape painter but fame had not spoilt him. He had won medals, the Emperor had supported him and bought his pictures, and the critics held his work in the highest esteem, but he remained untouched, virginal almost, in his simplicity.

Corot was immune to the seductive blandishments of fame. Although he enjoyed his popularity there was only one thing that he really wanted to do: to paint landscapes; and since fame did not hang like fruit from the trees in front of his easel, it was beside the point. Exactly the same applied to money and aesthetic speculation. The uninhibited pleasure that Corot took in his work, his unwavering faith in God and nature and the kindness with which he treated everyone he met were aspects of a character as impressive as it is rare. "An angel who smokes a pipe" was what the just, but usually caustic Degas once said of him.

But goodness, unless it leads to martyrdom or change, is not a quality that easily survives in the memory of future generations. Corot changed nothing and he died in his bed, on the 22nd of February, 1875, at the age of 79. He is one of the greatest painters of the nineteenth century but although he lived in the age of the camera and the interview, a period noted for its diaries and voluminous correspondence, the image he has left to posterity is not a powerful one.

When his name is mentioned the first thing that often comes to mind is a joke: of the three thousand pictures that Corot painted, it runs, some four thousand are now in America. This sally dates from before the first World War, when Corot's paintings were fashionable and much sought after in the United States, and while its humour may not have worn well, it is a useful reminder that Corot painted a great many canvases and that his work was (and is) easy to fake.

Neither of these facts have helped his reputation. It is hard to suppress a certain instinctive suspicion in front of any work by an artist who has been much faked. Then there is the sheer bulk of Corot's output. Most of the galleries of the world have at least one picture by him. Usually they have more. His paintings are highly predictable on the walls of any gallery, and they are also predictable in their character. Corot is one of the most repetitive of artists. It is easy to take him for granted. However satisfying his works may be, they do not have the startling variety or rarity value that sharpen appreciation and strengthen memory. No painting by Corot is liable to strike the beholder with that mingling of surprise and wonder, in the presence of something shatteringly clever and absolutely unique, that it is possible to feel in front of, shall we say, Vermeer's panoramic *View of Delft*.

There are other important reasons why "Papa" Corot does not strike us now as forcibly as he might. There is nothing, when all is said and done, like a colourful personality or an abundant sex life (preferably combined) to keep a figure from the past vividly before us. Henry VIII is well remembered; Henry VII is fairly easy to forget. Judged by these standards, Corot cuts but a poor figure. He had a strong and virtuous character but his personality was on the dull side. Apart from a few, fleeting escapades in his youth, his private life would seem to have been a model of respectability.

Corot lived for his work. And he was always prepared to talk about it. The chief drawback was that he had no real gift for words. Devoid of his living presence, of his vivacity and simple humour and of the forceful punctuation he would give them with the stem of his pipe, Corot's remarks have an uneasy ring. They often seem to us now exactly what they were not when they were made. "Never," Albert Dubuisson, who knew the artist, tells us, "was there a person less pontifical than he." But compared to the prose of Baudelaire, the *Journal* of Delacroix or the letters of Van Gogh, Corot's words often seem naive and sanctimonious.

Corot, then, is unlikely to appear in that vague, mental gallery of the illustrious dead that even the least historically minded carry in their memories. His temper was placid, his character admirable and his long life was unstained by great tragedy or grand vice. It would be easy to write a dull novel about Corot. A film would not be a commercial proposition.

The image of the sturdily built old man, with his white hair and ruddy complexion, weathered by a lifetime spent out of doors painting, puffing away at his pipe or singing snatches of opera, and still as innocently delighted with his own work as a boy who has just mastered a conjuring trick for the first time, somehow fades when it is set beside the tragic figure of Van Gogh or alongside that callous fanatic, Gauguin. Corot is almost like a maiden aunt who can never compete, in the family circle, with the nephews who have been round the world and suffered shipwreck, had dusky mulatto mistresses or been all but crucified for their faith. But then he was, at heart, both obstinate and timid and he never risked much.

Neither Corot's personality nor his way with words have helped his posthumous reputation. And since he did not move in intellectual circles he is not caught up in the fabric of memories that so many writers of the time have left us. He all but eluded the chilly pens of those omnivorous diarists, the Du Goncourts. Baudelaire admired his work but tells us virtually nothing about him as a man. The gregarious Delacroix seldom came across him. And when Balzac came to live near Corot at Ville d'Avray no close friendship was formed between them.

To add to our difficulties in seeing Corot vividly and coherently, there is the actual character of his work, with its clear division between what was thought suitable for public exhibition, in a bigoted and conservative art world, and the informal views and figures painted directly from nature. The *Forest of Fontainebleau* (plate 29) shown at the Salon of 1846, is the kind of elaborately finished, artifically composed studio landscape that the public, the critics and the juries of the Salon expected. *The Banks of the Cousin* (plate 22), which was painted in the first half of the 1840s, is a "snapshot" of nature and it is brushed in on the canvas with casual economy. To eyes accustomed to the Impressionists it has the virtues of freshness and spontaneity which the view of Fontainebleau conspicuously lacks. But the critics and the public whom Corot always tried to please, held fast to more traditional values. On to the new movements, the Realism of Courbet in the 1850s, and the Impressionism which began to emerge in the mid-1860s, they poured scorn and ridicule. Corot condoned Impressionism, and he was always ready to help struggling young painters privately, but he would never give his official support to the group. He hated factions of any kind. And by this time he was an old man, who knew that he belonged to another epoch.

Corot is, in fact, the last great European painter to have adopted a public and a private manner in what we now feel to be a detrimental sense. There are distinctly two sides to his work. His reputation has not suffered since the 1840s and yet he has never been admired for the whole of his art, in the way Degas or Monet or Braque are revered.

Up to the first World War, it was the long series of idyllic landscapes (they almost all date from after 1850), the vistas of lake and woodland with attendant figures that were most admired. These tend to be soft, lyrical and well bred. They are also coventional. A typical contemporary view of this aspect of Corot's art is to be found in the first act of Oscar Wilde's *An Ideal Husband* (1893). "But you have not seen my Corots yet," Sir Robert Chiltern remarks. "They are in the music room. Corots seem to go with music, don't they? May I show them to you?" But the blackmailing Mrs Cheveley wishes only to talk business. "I am not in the mood tonight," she replies, "for silver twilights, or rose-pink dawns."

Since the first World War taste in Corots has changed radically. The silvery glades, so aptly chosen by the Ballets Russe Company for the decor of a production of *Les Sylphides*, have given way, in the corridors of praise, to the brilliant studies of nature that were seldom exhibited and little known in the artist's lifetime. What Sickert dubbed "the big Bond Street Corot" has never really recovered its prestige.

The divided character of Corot's art makes it difficult for us to see it as a whole and the curious way that the passage of time has affected this division makes it even harder still. Rubens painted big official altarpieces and informal, private works simultaneously and they are in fundamentally the same style; the differences between his oil sketches and the full-size pictures are largely a matter of scale and degree of finish. The approach to subject matter, the organisation of the composition remain the same. But with Corot it is not so easy. Consider *The Bridge at Narni*. The sketch (plate 5), rapid, sparkling, almost scientific in its detached observation of light, looks not unlike an Impressionist picture of about 1875. The finished painting, on the other hand, is very carefully worked out (plate 6). It is rather like a Claude and it would not have been out of place at the Paris Salon of 1775.

With no other great artist of the nineteenth century, not even with the many-sided Turner, do we get so conflicting a sense of direction according to which aspect of his work we are examining. Corot of the sketches (plates 3, 7, 24) and the figure pieces (plates 9, 35, 51) seems to be welcoming the future, the Impressionists, the world of Utrillo even. But in the Salon pictures Corot is another man, as seemingly incapable as Orpheus of resisting the fatal temptation to look back.

It is, indeed, hard to know just where to place Corot. A famous exhibition held in Paris in 1925 was entitled "French Landscape from Poussin to Corot". From the art historical point of view, this span makes perfect sense. And yet another show, mounted in Paris in our own day could carry the equally coherent title "From Corot to Picasso".

Corot himself always recognised that there was a basic difference between the larger canvases produced in the studio and the smaller, less formal views that he invariably painted out of doors. But the gulf has been irrevocably widened and its character falsified by one crucial fact. And that fact is, quite simply, the Impressionist Revolution. The Impressionists have taught us that in art one theme is no better than another and that completion does not depend on degree of finish. In the directness of their observation, and in their avoidance of literary and narrative overtones, Corot's sketches from nature anticipate the Impressionists. It is these works that have been so firmly annexed by modern taste.

The result has been that we now regard them as being as important as the Salon paintings themselves. They have become, as it were, alternatives. Once we accept this, the two exhibition titles are valid. The explicit classical flavour of the Salon canvases links Corot to Poussin and Claude, while the fresh and uninhibited temper of the sketches is something that we readily admire in the pictures of Renoir or Manet. But the two kinds of painting that Corot produced were not, in fact, *alternatives* at all. They should really be seen as *different stages* in a complicated but single-minded process.

Although he exerted a profound influence on the Impressionists, Corot's whole approach to art was different. There were, as we shall see, a great many reasons for this. The most basic was one of age. Corot was a generation older than Pissarro and Monet and their confederates. He was born at the end of the eighteenth century and he was trained in the 1820s. And right up to the time of his death, Corot's work continued to reflect the complex aesthetic tensions which the Romantic Movement had introduced into art in the first quarter of the century.

Corot was born in Paris on July 16th, 1796, and he was christened Jean-Baptiste-Camille. He was always to prefer his third name of Camille. His father, Louis-Jacques Corot, was a cloth merchant of humble origin. His mother, on the other hand, came from a wealthier background. She was born Marie-Françoise Oberson and she was the daughter of a Versailles wine merchant. She owned property in Fribourg and brought with her on her marriage a dowry of ten thousand francs.

Madame Corot ran a haberdashery shop on the corner of the Quai d'Orsay and the Rue du Bac. This was a fashionable area during the First Empire and the little business did a brisk trade in accessories, ribbons and silks and the fabrics of the moment.

When he was seven, Corot was sent to the school of a M. Letellier in the Rue de Vaugirard. He boarded there until he was eleven. On December 15th, 1806, M. Corot secured for his son a scholarship to the Lycée at Rouen. The child went there in April, 1807, for what was to prove a period of five years. His *correspondent* (or "guardian on the spot") was a M. Sennegon, an old friend of his mother's. This rather melancholy individual was fond of communing with nature and he would often take the young Corot with him on his long walks. He was addicted to sunsets. The child was thus exposed, at an extremely impressionable age, to landscape and light; and not merely as a background but overcast with the reflective spirit of his companion.

Corot was never brilliant at school. He left Rouen at the end of June, 1812, without any scholastic honours. From 1812 to 1814 he was at a school in Poissy, where he studied, in his own words, "a form of rhetoric". Schooling ended when the lad was eighteen and the question of his future was naturally debated. He told his father that he wanted to study painting but M. Corot would not hear of it. So young Camille entered the family profession.

His first post was with a cloth merchant, M. Ratier, in the Rue de Richelieu, but he was soon dismissed for carelessness. The next job was with a M. Delalain in the Rue St Honoré and he stayed there until 1821. Corot made very little progress. He had no aptitude for business, and since he was shy and gauche, blushing when addressed, he could have been of only limited use in the shop. M. Delalain, in fact, began to use him more and more as a courier. But instead of concentrating on his errands, Corot would hang around the shop windows of the picture dealers or on the quays if he happened to see artists sketching.

For six years Corot wasted his time following a career he neither enjoyed nor carried through with any marked success. But he never complained, and forty years later, when he was reminiscing to biographers, and when his great reputation would have more than excused a few sharp words on the subject, he showed not the slightest trace of resentment. But then we are dealing with a man who had deep religious convictions, a strong sense of duty and an acquiescent, even submissive nature. Corot was always prepared to accept situations, artistic traditions, patterns of thought as they were.

In the winter of 1821-2, however, M. Corot finally relented. The change of heart was not quite as generous as it might at first have seemed. Camille's sister, Victoire-Anne, had died in September, 1821, and her allowance no longer had to be paid. M. Corot now felt able to allot his son fifteen hundred francs a year to pursue studies in which he could hardly do worse than he had done in the haberdashery trade.

No one thought Corot could manage on the sum allotted him, but they had not reckoned on the young man's complete lack of extravagance and his ability to concentrate once he found something that really suited him.

Corot immediately set to work on the banks of the Seine not far from the shop. Sometimes the girls who were employed there would stroll down to watch. From the very first, Corot was attracted by the idea of working in the open air. He also studied in the Louvre, but instead of paying proper attention to the masterpieces that hung on the walls he would sketch the copyists. He would also wander round the zoo drawing the animals.

In the early part of 1822, Corot began to take lessons from a now forgotten painter named Michallon. The contact was a crucial one. "I painted my first landscape direct from nature", he told the critic, Theodore Silvestre many years later, "at Arceuil under the eye of Michallon, whose only advice was to paint with scrupulous care everything that I saw before me."

Achille Etna Michallon was actually the same age as Corot but his experiences as an artist were already far more extensive. When they met, he was just back from a four-year stay in Italy, having won, in 1817, the newly instituted Academy prize for Historical Landscape. It was natural that Corot should have looked up to him and taken particular note of what he said. Michallon might well have pointed out the problems that beset a budding landscapist in France in the 1820s. How landscape was still rather looked down upon; how critics still followed the traditional, academic view that it was inferior to painted illustrations of uplifting themes taken from the Bible or classical history; and how the easiest way to soften these prejudices was to accept the traditional view of nature laid down in the seventeenth century, principally by Poussin and Claude.

By virtue of elaborate compositions, the idealisation of natural forms and the introduction of appropriate figures, these great artists had given to nature a moral tone, that sense or order and purpose that it so conspicuously lacked in its raw state. Careful finish was deemed equally important. These views dominated "establishment" thinking throughout the first half of the nineteenth century. The landscape painter was obliged to take them into the most serious consideration if he wanted to achieve any measure of official recognition and success. And often if he wanted to do no more than eat.

Michallon himself accepted these conditions and painted dull and lifeless classical compositions for public exhibition. So did Jean-Victor Bertin (1775-1842), Michallon's master, with whom Corot went on to study after Michallon's early death (September, 1822). Corot would seem to have regarded Bertin as his "official" teacher. In the Salon catalogues he always listed himself as *élève de V. Bertin.*

Corot, too, accepted the conditions of the day. And he never lost the desire to do well in official terms, to achieve success according to the accepted standards. Although he had a private income, and there was no need to sell or exhibit anything if he did not want to, he had a natural enough desire to make a success of his life. Since he was by nature timid and unquestioning, however, he accepted the crumbling edifice of early nineteenth-century aesthetics without demur. For only by conforming could he achieve the conventional success his largely conventional nature demanded. It is this whole-hearted acceptance of contemporary values that goes a long way towards explaining the "Salon Corot", the whole of his "official" career, *The Bridge at Narni* (plate 6) in its final form, *The Forest of Fontainebleau* (plate 29), *Homer and the Shepherds* (plate 28) and the *Danse des Nymphes* (plate 30). And it is this which most clearly sets him apart from the Impressionists.

There was no spirit of rebellion in Corot. He did not thrive, as Courbet did, on hostility. He always needed reassurance. And the atmosphere of tranquility that pervades almost all his works reflects, in his case, a mood, an envelope of feeling with which he found it necessary to surround himself in life.

But while early nineteenth-century conservative opinion still demanded finished (and if not classical, at least neo-Dutch) landscapes, art itself was slowly changing. The Romantic Movement, that enormous upsurge of emotionally charged philosophies which succeeded the Age of Reason, was casting its vivid shadows over every aspect of European art and thought.

One of the most important tenets of Romanticism was the exaltation of nature; as an experience for its own sake, as a source of wisdom and as an artistic inspiration. Throughout the greater part of the eighteenth century the scenic view had prevailed. But in the closing years people began to look at landscape and study nature more closely. The formalised vision of Gray's *Elegy* (1750) gives way to those intimate communings with nature that constitute Wordsworth's Ode, *Intimations of Immortality* (1807).

The eighteenth-century landscape painter had little desire to do much serious work out of doors because the formulas, the patterns of design he tended to follow were never meant to provide the actual facts of natural life. And when they did work in the open, a Fragonard or a Hubert Robert seldom did more than sketch with crayon or pencil. The Romantic Movement, on the other hand, began to exalt actual, personal experience in a way that the eighteenth century would have regarded as ill-bred and unformulated.

When Berlioz composed the *Corsair* overture, he was careful to provide a programme note, telling us how it had been inspired by a storm he had himself encountered on a voyage from Marseilles to Leghorn. In order to observe effects at first hand, Turner had himself tied to the mast during a storm at sea. And Constable often noted on the back of his oil sketches the date and actual time of day when they were made.

When he was in Italy, Corot's first master, Michallon, also painted direct studies out of doors. In these sketches (which include a handful of purely figure studies) he recorded the motifs, buildings and sky and land as they appeared to him, without any of the preconceptions suitable for the academic landscape he produced in the studio.

Even more important are the oil sketches (mostly in the Louvre) produced by Bertin's own master, Pierre Henry de Valenciennes (1750-1819) while he was in Rome in 1778-80. Once again we are given not emotive treatments of the great monuments but dispassionate records of different parts of the city, odd vistas of no intrinsic importance, chosen because Valenciennes was interested in seeing, for example, how the light falls on a roof at different times of the day. In his treatise, *Eléments de Perspective pratique à l'usage des Artistes* (published in 1800; a second, enlarged edition came out in 1820) he advises the student to "paint the same view at different hours of the day so as to observe the changes that the light produces in forms". Valenciennes had a strong feeling for the unifying effects of light on colour and attempted to reproduce a variety of atmospheric conditions.

But in spite of their quality, these were undercover works and they were not meant for exhibition. What Valenciennes did show the world were carefully finished landscapes in the vein of Claude and Poussin. Just as he wrote in his treatise that landscape painting could only achieve the dignity of historical painting when it conformed to the principles of Ideal Beauty and included antique, biblical or mythological figures to give it an heroic quality. For his pains, Valenciennes was awarded membership of the Academy in 1787. He was a success.

The work of both Michallon and Valenciennes reflects the complex pressures, the uneasy combination of new forces and old prejudices that were in operation at the end of the eighteenth century and during the first quarter of the nineteenth century. Romanticism was a deep-rooted growth that flourished, and flourished abundantly, but it grew along a trellis of decaying ideas and assumptions left over from the past. As if in tacit recognition of the new importance attached to nature, the Academy might, in 1816, create a new prize for landscape; but they made certain that it would be for "Historical Landscape".

In the early nineteenth century the landscape painter was unable to express, in a form suitable for the official exhibition, and acceptable to a conservative public, all the new attitudes to nature. These, therefore, had of necessity to find an outlet in the preliminary stages of picture-making, which came to assume greater and greater importance for the artist. Before nature, Hubert Robert and Fragonard had been content to use pencils and crayons. But now the artist was working out of doors in oils. The portable pocket book was no longer enough. Now the painter set up his easel and surrounded himself with all his tubes and brushes.

It is this rather strained and in many ways contradictory pattern that Corot found in the careers of his teachers and contemporaries such as Michallon and Valenciennes. He accepted it, modelled his own practice on it and stuck to it throughout his life.

Until 1825, Corot worked away in his native France. He concentrated on small, informal landscapes on which he would work out of doors. He travelled extensively, visiting and working in Fontainebleau, Dieppe, Arques, Le Havre, Honfleur, Caen, Granville and Roches de Ham. He also worked at Ville d'Avray, near Paris, where his father had owned a property since 1817. Very few paintings from these student years have survived at all. Those that have (such as plate 2), reveal the same kind of direct observation and feeling for the unity of light that Michallon and Valenciennes display in their oil sketches. The connection is close and is useful evidence against the often repeated idea that Corot was a pioneer in his work out of doors.

Up to about the middle of the nineteenth century, no artistic education was thought to be complete without a visit to Italy. Rome was then what Paris was to become — and remain until 1939 — and what New York is perhaps today: the goal and the centre. Corot was in close touch with classicising painters who had themselves been in Italy and he was naturally anxious to make the trip himself. In 1825, his father agreed. The only condition he imposed was that his son should leave behind a self-portrait. This is the small canvas now in the Louvre (plate 1). Seated on a cane-bottomed chair, the young man of 29 stares out at the spectator with an expression that is both serious and alert. The gaze is direct. And so is the technique. The forms are blocked in with solid areas of colour. The textures are thick, even rather pasty, evidence of a still inexperienced hand. But in other respects, the portrait is surprisingly mature. The simplification of the forms and the unity of the colouring, of the tones, are impressive and are superior to anything that Michallon or Valenciennes had done. Michallon's oil sketches are finicky and he was prone to include an almost topographical amount of detail. Valenciennes was interested in the fall of light, and its optical effect on coloured objects, but his command of tone was often unsteady.

In November, 1825, Corot set off for Italy with the painter Behr, a fellow student at Bertin's. Corot had been working for three years but he had, so far, very little to show for it. He had worked hard but had exhibited nothing in public. Indeed, it would not appear that he had yet attempted anything on the grand scale. He had spent time in the Louvre, but the masterpieces there had not roused in him any spirit of emulation; Corot had no sense of rivalry and, unlike Turner, he never tried to beat the great artists of the past on their own ground.

The two young artists finally reached Rome in December of 1825. Corot immediately took a small room near the Spanish Steps. He was to remain in Italy for just under three years and the work pattern he set for himself was to serve for the rest of his life. From spring to autumn he would travel about and work out of doors. In the winter he would spend most of his time in the studio, working up larger, finished pictures from his sketches. In the spring and summer of 1826, Corot travelled about with Behr. They worked principally in the Sabine mountains, visiting Civita Castellana, Viterbo, Castel Sant-Elia, Narni and Papigno. In November, Corot was in the Alban hills, at Marino,

Albano, Ariccia, Frascati and Nemi, while in December he was working at Tivoli. He followed a similar pattern in 1827. In the spring of 1828, Corot visited Naples, Capri and Ischia. After a return trip to Rome in the early summer he went on, in September, to Venice. It was from here that he set off for Paris, which he finally reached in October.

Rome is more than a place, it is an experience, and a visitor's reactions are more than usually indicative of character. To Winckelmann, the great German exponent of classicism, Rome was the ultimate goal and his greatest reward. "One gets spoilt here", he writes in 1763, "but God owed me this: in my youth I suffered too much." Whistler was in Rome in February, 1899, but he was not, perhaps, really in the mood; he described it as "a bit of an old ruin alongside a railway station where I saw Mrs Potter Palmer".

Corot was the least flippant of men, and he stayed a good deal longer, but his reaction was, in some respects, similar to that of Whistler. He was hardly conscious of the city's larger claims on the mind and the imagination. Corot had no real interest in the past. He did not go near the Sistine Chapel (one of the pinnacles of the classical tradition that his finished works would always continue to support), until his third visit to Italy in 1843. What struck him most forcibly was the light. "It is always fine weather", we find him writing from Rome in the spring of 1826, "but, on the other hand, this sun casts a light which makes me despair. I become aware of the utter impotence of my palette. Honestly, there are days when I feel like throwing the whole thing to the devil". His reactions were not poetic or philosophic but technical.

There were, from the first, problems. Corot quickly discovered that the drawback of life as a subject is that it won't stay still. "Some children were sitting on the steps of a church", he reminisced to Silvestre years later, apropos of his first trip to Italy, "I would begin again. Then their mother would call them. My notebook would be filled with bits of noses, foreheads and locks of hair. I decided that in future I would not go back home without having accomplished a complete work; and for the first time I tried drawing in the mass — rapid drawing — the only drawing possible. I set myself to take in a group at a glance; if it stayed in place for only a short time, well, at least I had got its character, its general unconscious character. If it remained longer, I was able to fill in more detail."

People get up and go away, the sun moves, shadows change, colours alter. Nothing is absolutely still or the same for very long, but some things, notably at a distance, change, or seem to change, more slowly. Their appearance is more amenable to scrutiny and if observed at the same time of day and in the same kind of weather they can come to seem almost fixed. Corot quickly came to accept the principles that these facts imply. He preferred, as he was always to prefer, a distant grouping of his main subject: *La Trinité* (plate 4), the *Cathedral of Chartres* (plate 11), *Florence from the Boboli Gardens* (plate 18), *The Bridge at Mantes* (Louvre, Paris). There is an instructive story on this point in George Moore's *Modern Painting*. One day, Moore came upon the aged painter "in front of his easel in a pleasant glade. After admiring his work,

1 STREAM IN THE WOOD OF CIVITA CASTELLANA

2 MORNEX: JUNE 1842

3 PORTRAIT OF A WOMAN

I ventured to say: 'What you are doing is lovely, but I cannot find your composition in the landscape before us'. He said, 'My foreground is a long way ahead'. And sure enough, nearly two hundred yards away, his picture rose out of the dimness of the dell, stretching a little beyond the vista into the meadow."

At a distance objects not only seem to hold their appearance exactly, but the very space that separates them from the eye serves to simplify their forms. This simplification of form was equally important to Corot. He came to cherish, by virtue of his classical training and a certain instinctive feeling, wholeness of form and wholeness of effect. His landscapes are often informal but they are never intimate. Constable could delight in the poppies that grew by a wall but Corot never fastened on the tiny fragment of nature, just as he never cared for a minute, pre-Raphaelite finish. He used to grow quite angry with his brother-in-law, who was fond of pictures to which one could, with advantage, apply a magnifying glass. "According to his idea", Corot said, "one would have to look at landscape through a telescope and turn painting into astronomy."

It is symptomatic of Corot's desire for a vision at once whole and simplified that he always tended to ignore the foreground as an element to be recorded. What he often did was vaguely to suggest its character, in subdued tones that are in harmony with the main background elements. When he does treat the foreground more elaborately (as in the *View of Soissons*, plate 12), it often appears jarringly artificial. It was not an issue that interested him and he was, as a consequence, quite willing to accept traditional formulas; in this case devices deriving, ultimately, from Claude and seventeenth-century Dutch masters.

Once he reached the Mediterranean world, Corot was also quick to realise that light does not strengthen bright colours; it bleaches them. In this one fact, more than in perhaps any other single aspect of his craft, Corot found the point of entry into a world of satisfying pictorial form. By adding white lead to his pigments he was able to achieve a more accurate record of appearances dimmed by the brilliance of the Mediterranean sun. The introduction of white into all his colours also provided him with the equivalent of a key in music, a unifying factor binding the notes of colour into an unassailably harmonious pictorial melody. In the *View of the Forum* (plate 3), the pinkish browns of the stone, the sage greens of the foliage, the purplish shadows, each and every colour fulfils this double function. It describes, with unparalleled accuracy, a visual fact, but it also contributes, without any sacrifice to that accuracy, a unit to the pictorial harmony.

The incredible accuracy of Corot's observation was really a natural endowment of his sight; it is not teachable. And fine though the sketches of Valenciennes and Michallon are, they do not have it. The principles that Corot evolved in Italy were to serve him wherever he set down his easel in the open air. And having learnt to achieve harmony and accuracy in the dramatic atmospheric conditions of the Mediterranean, he found it relatively easy to cope with northern Europe, with its naturally unifying layers of mist and more restricted colour ranges. *Saint-André-en-Morvan* (plate 23) is an incredible (and still quite accurate) study in interrelated shades of green.

But while one should always emphasise Corot's uncanny eye for the accurate tone, for knowing just the right shade of buff for a wall or the absolutely correct purplish grey for a shadow, it does not follow that his pictures are accurate after the fashion of a photograph. Corot's range of colour *was* restricted — and this once more contrasts him with the Impressionists — and it was not until late in life that he had any wish to reproduce a familiar phenomenon in life, the sudden *lunge* of colour, in a dress or a vehicle, that quite dominates a scene. His methods were different. "It has seemed important", he wrote, "in preparing a picture (assuming a white canvas) by indicating the most vigorous (dark) values and to continue in orderly manner up to the lightest. Between the dark and the light I should allow twenty gradations; thus will your picture be established with order." Silvestre, who knew Corot in later life, noted how he would run "an unquiet eye over every part of the canvas before putting a touch in place, sure that it does no violence to the general effect. If he makes haste he may become clumsy and rough, leaving here and there inequalities of impasto. These he afterwards removes with a razor."

Anything that might destroy the right unity was played down. In the *View of Florence from the Boboli Gardens* (plate 18), for example, he toned down considerably the bright reddish brown of the Cathedral dome. Corot was also quite capable of making adjustments to the actual shape and grouping of buildings in a scene. In a *View of the Forum* (about 1845, Private Collection) he reduced the number of the domes, spaced out those he did retain, simplified façades and made the tower of the Capitol more slender than it is in reality.

In the course of his long career Corot painted in hundreds of places, but the type of view that he favoured was relatively limited. It was invariably an inland subject. He had little or no serious interest in the sea. Partly because water, being translucent and sparkling, did not readily lend itself to the opaque textures that white-mixed pigments tend to create. Only in later life, when his style had become more transparent and luminous, did Corot regularly begin to introduce sheets of still and pearly water. But in his earlier works he rejected the sparkling highlights and transparent glazes that were so popular with his contemporaries. The texture of his sketches is thick and porous, not unlike early Rembrandt.

And unlike Rubens and Constable, Corot never looked the midday sun directly in the face. Partly because it would have constituted, like the single flash of powerful colour, a dominating chord. And partly because it belonged to a whole range of natural effects that did not appeal to his artist's temperament. Corot seldom represents nature in movement. *The Gust of Wind* (plate 46) is a rarity in his work. Constable is the master of clouds and wind and turbulent skies; and Turner created a whole series of masterpieces on the themes of the snowstorm and the wild sea.

The main reason why Constable and Turner were able to see nature in so many moods was because their sharp powers of observation were combined with imaginative faculties of a high order. This quality of imagination not only introduced into their work a larger dimension, a sense of nature as the "chief organ of sentiment", but it also allowed them to guess. For some element of guesswork must invariably take place when one is trying to pin down anything so fluctuating as a snowstorm or a rough sea. Turner's *Fire at Sea* (National Gallery, London) would be an impossibility in terms of Corot's style.

To Corot himself, with his literal mind and, in a certain sense, naive standards of accuracy, the idea of guesswork would have seemed almost immoral. He liked his subjects, no matter whether they were the *Church of St Paterne at Orleans* (plate 26), *M. Pivot on Horseback* (plate 33) or the girls he posed in exotic costumes in his studio (plates 47, 48) to have the virtues of still-life. This way he was able to relate exactly a red in front of him to a red in his palette, a shadow with a painted shadow, and so on.

There is one further reason why nature in movement did not appeal to Corot. It was not part of the tradition he accepted in his youth. The essential qualities in the work of Bertin, Michallon and Valenciennes are harmony and stability; and these are the qualities of Poussin and Claude. Even their unexhibited oil sketches from nature have a serenity and equilibrium that make similar works by Constable and Turner seem, by comparison, agitated and fragmentary.

While he was in Italy, Corot was busy working out of doors but there still lingered at the back of his mind, broad and perpetual, like a rule of conduct learnt in childhood, a sense of his larger duty. That duty of which the anonymous critic of the 1824 Salon was so aware when he asked: "What would become of the landscapist's art if, through over-timidity, he feared to burst into the domain of history? What poetry, what high inspiration, could fire him in his labours?"

Corot sent two pictures to the Salon of 1827. Of these only *The Bridge at Narni* (plate 6) has survived. It is very different in character from the sketch, which is a "snapshot" of nature, and looks like a Claude. It is close in style to the work of Caruelle d'Aligny, a painter of classical landscapes whom Corot met in Rome. He always considered that what he had learnt from d'Aligny had been crucial for his development as an artist. *The Bridge at Narni* received a brief but favourable mention in the press. The sketch Corot kept in his studio.

In October, 1828, Corot was back in Paris. He brought with him all the sketches that he had made in Italy. He had grown a beard which his father ordered him to shave off at once. He did so. But he was quite stubborn when it came to the question of marriage. He had his painting. He was wedded to Art. "All I really want to do in life", we find him writing to Abel Osmond from Italy in August, 1826, "and without deviation . . . is to paint landscapes. This firm resolution will prevent me from forming any serious attachments. That is to say, in marriage."

And Corot never did marry. This strict adherence to what would, in most cases, amount to no more than a flamboyant pledge of youth is symptomatic of a character at once conservative, stubborn and unquestioning. Corot preserved a peasant-like resistance to change. He also had the simple man's unyielding faith in habit. At the very end of his life he was still using the small bedroom, in the family house at Ville d'Avray, that he had been allotted as a youth. The past was all about him. The finished version of *The Bridge at Narni* (plate 6), his first official success painted forty years before, hung over the bed in his Paris studio. And he always kept a large proportion of all his sketches from nature; they formed the chief decoration of his various studios. Often he would buy back specimens that had, for one reason or another, strayed from his possession.

These aspects of Corot's character have an important bearing on his career as an artist. As soon as the parental opposition had been broken down, in the early 1820s, Corot had rushed out and set up his easel on the banks of the Seine. In September, 1873, plagued by flies and the dreadful smell and the distraction of curious spectators, he was setting up his easel in the tanneries at Mantes (plate 49). Like a priest, for whom prayers lose none of their value through repetition, Corot continued to paint from nature until the very last weeks of his life. There were, of course, modifications as the years went by, softenings of form and colour, but the essentials remained precisely what they had been in his youth: to provide a truthful and harmonious record of what he saw in front of him.

Corot's career reveals an impressive continuity of purpose and a continual satisfaction with the same kind of results that is more remarkable still. The similarity between *Le Petit Chaville* (plate 2) and a late work such as the *Souvenir de Saintry* (plate 50), painted fifty years later in 1874, is strong and it appears even more striking if one compares the earliest and latest works of a Monet, a Renoir or a Cézanne.

Although he jealously guarded his independence, Corot still liked an atmosphere of sympathy and human warmth. At the same time he imposed his own strict conditions. The result was that he tended to make friends with fellow painters who were willing to accompany him on his painting expeditions. That way he gained all the advantages of friendship without having to put up with any of its distractions. In 1829, for example, we find him going off to Normandy and Brittany with Rémy, a landscapist whom he had first met in the studio of Bertin.

Corot always made a point of spending the good months of the year, from spring to autumn, painting out of doors, but much as he enjoyed this there was always underneath a certain longing for home. In 1829 we find him writing in a notebook: "I shall return, I hope, towards the end of August and embrace the family I adore." Corot's father died in 1847; and then, until his mother's death in 1851, he did not travel at all. After his parents were dead, Corot relied on a series of substitute families. There were the Roberts at Mantes, the Dutilleux menage at Arras and the Bovy family at Gruyères in Switzerland; and others. But wherever he went, it was on the implicit understanding that he could paint undisturbed.

During the 1830s, Corot worked extremely hard. He travelled and painted in dozens of places and during this decade he also increased the size of his sketches before nature. In 1834 he again visited Italy but the trip was cut short. He received news of his father's illness and hurried home.

During this decade Corot made every attempt to consolidate his public reputation. He loved the act of painting, the sheer process of ensnaring the view, but he also had a sense of completion. Leonardo da Vinci drifted and dreamed and left things only half finished. This would have shocked Corot, who believed strongly in the morality of work. He was stable, conscientious and persistent. This applied to his individual pictures. In the spring of 1868 he stayed for a few days at a country house at Brunoy, near Paris. Albert Dubuisson, a member of his host's family, recalled that "while talking and puffing away at his pipe he kept throwing, from time to time, a glance at his study. Suddenly he rushed forward to his palette and snatched up his brushes, crying 'Ah! the brigand! the scoundrel! he shan't escape me a second time. I've got him!' Seating himself quickly at his easel, he squeezed out a tube of white and started to model on his canvas a big white sunlit cloud that was just appearing above the mass of greenery and foliage that formed part of his picture. 'We are just like crafty fishermen,' he added as he made rapid strokes with the brush, 'we have to seize the propitious moment to make the fish fall into our net.'"

And this also applied to his career as a whole. The finished landscape suitable for the Salon was, for Corot, the natural conclusion of an activity that he always tried to keep well within the framework of traditional practice and public approval. It is typical of him that when the *Burning of Sodom* was refused for the Salon of 1843, instead of forgetting all about it, he should submit it again the following year. And, furthermore, as if feeling that its rejection had somehow left a scar on it, like the marks of a disease, he should repaint it and show it at the Salon of 1857.

At the Salon of 1831, Corot showed *La Cervara* (plate 8), while at the exhibition of 1833, where he was awarded a second class medal, *The Forest of Fontainebleau* was highly praised by Lenormant in *Le Temps* as the most perfect landscape in the show. At the Salon of 1835, Corot exhibited the enormous *Hagar in the Wilderness* (plate 17), in which the scenery was based on sketches made at Narni and Terni. Though it remained unsold (Corot kept it until his death), the *Hagar* received a good deal of attention. A lithograph of it appeared in *Le Charivari* (May 29th, 1835), while the critic Schoelcher, writing in the *Revue de Paris*, prophesied that, if he continued in this vein, Corot would become one of the great names in French painting.

Corot sold virtually nothing and was frequently criticised for the lack of variety in his tones but he was not in the least beaten. Critics might object and he might be badly hung at exhibitions ("Oh dear," he would exclaim on seeing where they had put his pictures, "I am in the catacombs") but he went on doggedly. At the Salon of 1837, he showed the *St Jerome* (Church of Ville d'Avray) which was admired for its "elevated feeling" but criticised for the monotony of the scenery and for the "pale and uniform" colour.

Right at the end of the 1830s, however, Corot began to enjoy the first real rewards for all his efforts. He was becoming well known and his style familiar. Theophile Gautier actually wrote a sonnet around his picture of *Evening* and it was published in *La Presse*. And at the Salon of 1840 the *Flight into Egypt* was hung in the much coveted Salon Carré. The painting was much admired. Perhaps even more exciting for Corot was the first purchase of his work by the state. *Le Petit Berger* (also shown at the Salon of 1840) was acquired for the museum at Metz for 1500 francs. When Corot's father heard the news he was amazed. "And you really think that Camille has talent?" he asked one of his son's friends.

The success continued. Corot was now an established figure. The critic of *L'Artiste* could write of him as "one of the most serious and respected names in landscape painting". In 1842 the *Site d'Italie* was acquired by the State for the Museum at Avignon. When the *Burning of Sodom* (Louvre) was rejected by the committee for the Salon of 1843, protests were raised all over the place. Even Louis Philippe lent his support. Camille Pelletan, writing in *La Sylphide*, was full of indignation that such shabby treatment could be meted out to "Corot, our greatest landscape painter . . . a classical talent, nourished on the masters, from Titian to Poussin."

In his account of the Salon of 1845, Baudelaire could roundly proclaim: "At the head of the modern school of landscape stands M. Corot." On the 5th of July, 1846, Corot was awarded the Legion of Honour.

By the mid 1840s Corot had achieved the official success towards which he had been working for twenty years. He had sold, it is true, very little, but in the early 1850s collectors began to take a serious interest in his work. And so, naturally, did the dealers. He accepted offers made by Beugniet, Bourges and Martin, who were showing his pictures in their windows in the Rue Lafitte. One offer he refused, however, came from a dealer called Strottin. He wanted Corot to paint pictures "as remote from nature as possible".

This offer was no doubt based on a shrewd assessment of public taste and of Corot's own exhibited work, with its artifice and consciously poetic effects, and it was, in the circumstances, an understandable one. What would have shocked Corot was the idea that he should start out, that he should begin, with the intention of producing an effect that was, for him, no more than a residue. The big pictures, the *Hagar* or the *St Jerome* for example, were all carefully worked up from studies made out of doors. Each scene was meant to be a convincing account of nature in a relevant mood or condition. They might *look* artificial but that had not been at all the intention. Corot had great creative integrity. Many of his larger pictures painted in the studio carried the prefix "Souvenir" (plates 43, 44), in their titles. It is as if the artist wished to make absolutely clear, not only to the public but to himself as well, that since they had not been produced in front of the "motif" but from sketches they could never claim to be more than memories.

Time has undoubtedly widened the gap between Corot's "Salon" work and his out-door studies, but this gap was always there and it was always a very real one. Sometimes the gulf seems so wide that the only possible way to bridge it is to admit that Corot was a hypocrite. "Poussin indeed!" he once burst out in the middle of a discussion. "Grand lines, the classical — I don't care a jot for them. I live in the woods." A charming sentiment, to be sure, but one that is hard to square with, shall we say, *Homer and the Shepherds* (plate 28) or the *Danse des Nymphes* (plate 30).

But Corot was neither a hypocrite nor a fool. And the dichotomy begins to dissolve once we relate the nature and limitations of Corot's talent to his actual personality.

Although it does, of course, support a view of his work that is very largely a modern one, it is still safe to claim, as a fact, that the aesthetic experience Corot treasured more than anything else was working out of doors. It was the greatest experience he knew and in the winter he would pine for the spring so that he could be out again. He adored the countryside, and since he was deeply religious, nature gained an added dimension from being a product of God's handiwork. And out of doors he did not have to think about aesthetics. Pinning down what he saw in front of him satisfied his basically simple urge, essentially that of a craftsman, to do something accurately and have it grow in accuracy, stroke by stroke, as he worked.

Before nature Corot responded with a kind of irrestistible accuracy and he was able to combine this with a high degree of purely aesthetic harmony. In art, if not always in life, harmony is power. It gives us control over the chaotic materials and ingredients that are all about us. Standing in the centre of Piccadilly Circus, we are assaulted from every side, by sounds, smells, sights, movement, noise and conflict. Instinctively, we half withdraw; and Piccadilly Circus becomes a blurred impression. In front of the *View of Villeneuve-lès-Avignon* (plate 19) we do not withdraw. The senses burgeon in the assuring atmosphere which a single point of view creates. For we are only told one thing about the town: how it looks under light; the impression it conveys from a distance on a fine day. The structure of the buildings or the rocks, what kind of life goes on in the once papal city, all other considerations are swept aside. The picture is a record of a distant group of buildings treated as if they were still-life.

This mixture of the harmonious and the dispassionate is something Corot shares with Vermeer and — though to a lesser extent — with Chardin. It is an unusual combination and one that is, moreover, puzzling and not a little frustrating. In front of a Corot painted from nature, the exquisite harmony of the colouring and the incredible accuracy of the observation interract and quicken the senses to expect something more; some message, some concern with the human condition. But it is not there. At first it is hard to believe that anyone who says things so well really has nothing to say?

The famous view of Chartres (plate 11) illustrates the point well enough. The cathedral is seen, as Corot usually preferred to see his main "motifs", from a distance. In the foreground are a hillock and building stores. One of the greatest of the cathedrals in the Gothic manner, which for the Romantic generation meant something evocative, mysterious and exciting, is stripped of all mystery and association. Nor is there the slightest sense, as there is in Constable's view of Salisbury Cathedral from across the meadows, of a larger context, of any possible relationship between this supreme symbol of man's faith and surrounding nature. Thinking once about Cambridge, E. M. Forster could see, side by side, a ladder, a handcart, a small heap of sand and King's College Chapel. He immediately drew a symbolic conclusion. Corot would not have done so. "I paint", he once said, "a woman's breast as I'd paint a common container of milk . . . The form and the contrasts of value — that's what's essential."

The true nature of Corot's talent was technical. And he fully justifies the comment that Cézanne once made about Monet — "He is only an eye, but my God what an eye!" The particular character of his work depends, very precisely, on his personality, which acted like a steel corset, providing both unlimited support and crippling confinement.

It is Corot's simplicity and candour and total lack of imagination, taken in conjunction with his phenomenal powers of observation, that gives to his sketches their quality of radiant emptiness. And it is the same candour and simplicity, combined with a complacent delight in his own skill, of which he never tired, that enabled him to create a vast number of works in a style which suffered only one fundamental alteration in half a century. Corot does not develop through a series of clearly defined stylistic phases. There is only one great *caesura*, in the 1840s, when he passed from a bright, rather blond tonality and firm modelling towards a looser handling of paint and a more silvery colour scale.

Corot grew up in an age that expected an artist to tell the spectator something about a landscape in addition to the mere facts of nature. That it was noble, perhaps, and reflected a benign deity, or picturesque, or merely that it was a haven, a pleasant place to live in. But in this exercise — in which so many lesser talents have excelled — Corot never really succeeded. For in his heart of hearts he did not see landscape in these terms. He did not care whether a landscape was pleasant to live in. Though he loved nature dearly, he loved her with a kind of passionate disregard. What he was always testing was his skill. He would never take this for granted and stay in one place and think and think about one particular view like Cézanne. Having new sites to paint constantly sharpened the simple pleasures of accurate delineation.

Corot had no imagination and he had nothing to "say". But since his orthodox nature accepted the whole tradition of classical landscape painting in which he was trained, he was obliged to involve himself with broader issues: ideas; conceptions; visions. And since he had a concrete mind that appreciated clear and visible facts, it was the clear and visible apparatus of the classical tradition that he took over into his own works: the isolated distance; the Claudian curtain of trees; mythological figures and poetic effects of light. One is inclined to think that he would have been incapable of appreciating that, from the formal point of view, Cézanne or Seurat could be as classical as Claude and Poussin.

Constable and Delacroix were much concerned, throughout their careers, with

4 WOOD WITH SEATED WOMAN

5 LANDSCAPE

6 PORTRAIT OF A WOMAN

7 LA TOILETTE

carrying through a visual idea from the initial sketch to the finished work. There is a fundamental continuity in their practice and thinking. Corot's position was more complex. Although he laboured in the studio every winter on paintings that would be suitable for the Salon, the most significant aesthetic experience that he knew was working out of doors. It is not always noticed but it is precisely to this that nearly all his remarks on art refer. "One should go to the fields and not to pictures," he once remarked. "Work hard and work steadily," we find him writing to Berthe Morisot in 1864, "don't think too much about Papa Corot; nature is a still better adviser." "Vive la conscience, vive la simplicité" was a favourite remark. "You must interpret nature with entire simplicity, and according to your personal sentiment, disregarding what you know of the old masters or of contemporaries. Only in this way will you do work of real feeling."

Violent incongruities will retreat before the bright, advancing spear of intelligence but under the canopy of a faith they can exist happily side by side. The highly intelligent and analytic Degas painted history pictures at the beginning of his career but abandoned the genre when he realised that it was not consonant with his talent. But Corot could see nothing wrong with, on the one hand, advising artists to study nothing but nature and, with the other, producing *La Danse des Bergères* (plate 40). His very faith and delight in working out of doors sustained him, carrying him, as a great religious conviction will carry a man, into areas in which it is no longer strictly relevant.

Inseparable from this faith in nature was an amazing capacity for acceptance. The lack of curiosity was monumental. Corot never read newspapers and he took little, if any, interest and no part in political life. When the revolution broke in 1830 he went away to Chartres and painted the cathedral (plate 11). The 1848 revolution passed him by. At the Universal Exhibition of 1867, which immediately inspired the Du Goncourts and Flaubert to reflect on larger issues, Corot, after making a few extremely naive remarks in front of the armaments, hurried on, with evident relief, to his own works which were on display. "How I love my *Soir*," he remarked. There was perhaps no art that Corot cared for quite as much as his own.

There was a powerful streak of complacency in Corot but it was not entirely that. His pictures became, it is no exaggeration to say, something that he could love. Obedient to a regime of never ceasing work, it was perhaps inevitable that some of the thwarted tenderness of this obstinate but naturally affectionate man should be transferred to the work itself.

Stubborn he certainly was, orthodox, candid and naive, with a craftsman's delight in his own skill. A keen critic of his own work only in its details, he regarded the overall results with a self-indulgence that kept him satisfied with the same effects for years. He attached to working out of doors an importance out of all proportion to its place in the technique of classical landscape. And here we may note a fundamental difference between Corot and contemporaries such as Constable and Delacroix. Corot did not have initial inspirations that were elaborated into large, finished pictures. The big

Salon pictures were nearly always made up *afterwards* from sketches that had been done with *no* precise intention in mind. It was largely a matter of fitting various suitable parts together according to a compositional formula. Except in one or two special cases, such as the large *Baptism* of 1845 where the figures needed special attention, Corot did not first have an idea and then work out all the details in special studies. The relationship between the sketch and the composed studio picture is not, as with Constable and Delacroix, direct and organic but indirect and pre-fabricated.

Corot was lacking in real imagination, and it is this deficiency, more than anything else, that has cast so suspect a shadow over his career. Because so many of the finished landscapes look derivative and tiresomely artificial, it is easy to assume that the motives that lay behind their creation were equally discoloured. But this is very far from the case. Corot's life was stitched from within by his belief in the morality of work, artistic tradition, and harmonious effects of colour. It is this stitching that held his career together so firmly; and it died with him. To posterity the *œuvre* will never seem quite right: adrift, as it were, at the seams. For the morality of work, about which Corot was always talking, and his silent acceptance of the classical tradition are of little ultimate interest to future generations, who are more concerned with imaginative issues which he did not discuss and in which, it is reasonable to assume from the evidence, he took very little interest.

It is hard not to feel that the orthodox streak in Corot's character must have been strengthened by his experiences as a youth. The six enforced years he had spent in the family trade must have left him with a burning desire to succeed in terms that his conventional and unsympathetic father would thoroughly appreciate. Corot's phenomenal industry is partly explained by the shadow of paternal opposition that lay over his life until 1847. He never stopped. He was always working, as if he were constantly seeking to prove that he was not wasting his time. The notebooks and recorded sayings are always harping on the theme of "Ceaseless work, either executing or observing. An invulnerable conscience."

Corot had a strong sense of filial duty and he was nervous of his father but he would not give in, preferring to accept the hostility as a fact of life. M. Corot's reactions to his son's career might seem comic if they did not reveal a narrow mind and an unforgiving nature. When he heard that Camille had been awarded the Legion of Honour (1846) he at first refused to believe it, thinking for a moment that it had been given to himself.

The relationship between Corot's outdoor work and the finished studio canvases is often, as we have seen, a strained one and the gulf has been widened by the shift in taste from the one to the other. But there are important, if rather subtle connections that should not be overlooked. The precepts of his classical training, interacting with the less positive elements in his character and personality, imposed severe restrictions on what Corot did, and did not, look at and paint when he was in the open air.

In *Rain, Wind and Steam* (National Gallery, London), Turner produced the first masterpiece of the Railway Age. Railways play a small but vital role in Tolstoy's novel *Anna Karenina*. And Monet painted them. But there are no railways in Corot. Just as there is no proper snow, another Impressionist subject. Snow is unclassical; it is not to be found in Claude or Poussin. And one need hardly stress that railways do not come within the scope of Virgil or Theocritus.

Corot had no sense of *modernité*. His nature was, it is true, acquiescent but his resistance to what he did not want to absorb was monumental. It had the strength of pure indifference. Delacroix was intellectual and he was always taking in ideas that, in the event, he might either accept or reject. Corot, who was not intellectual, had a great capacity for ignoring things. The modern world as such meant nothing to him. And he could not see, as Baudelaire or Courbet could see, that it might be heroic too.

Géricault, Delacroix, Constable and Turner all painted famous contemporary events. The world of the Impressionists is full of cafés and streets and boating parties. And Monet once filled a garden, to the scale of a seventeenth-century altarpiece, with nothing but women in billowing summer dresses. The figures in Corot's landscapes are, by comparision, shadowy beings. They tend to be either plainly theatrical nymphs or dimly realised farm workers. They are appropriate but one is not made to feel that they are altogether relevant. This is almost certainly because Corot himself never *saw* people in a landscape. They were too liable to move. Along with the foreground they belonged to the class of tasteful necessities. And yet, looked at from another point of view, this apparent weakness is but one more symptom of his integrity. Corot was bad at guessing; he did not want to guess and he was not going to pretend that he did.

The implicit assumptions that Corot came to make about landscape, dictated, in the most obvious sense, what he should not paint. But they also exercised a positive influence on his composition and colouring. It is known that when he was working out of doors, he would often shift about before finally settling in front of a vista that really pleased him. Once, while he was working in the forest at Fontainebleau, a spectator, who had been watching him at work for some time, asked: "But where, monsieur, do you see that splendid tree you've put there?" Corot took his pipe from his mouth and without turning round pointed with the stem at an oak tree *behind him*.

Corot was not, as Baudelaire rightly said, a colourist but a harmonist. The relationship between colours was of more importance to him than their hues. This feeling for harmony was, of course, instinctive. He did not say to himself: I must not have a strong red chimney in my picture. His feelings prevented him from *seeing* a jarring shade of red. "We don't see in the same way," he once said to his pupil, Pissarro "You see green and I see silver and blond." This bias does not, however, impair the truth of his art because Corot recognised, implicitly, that in art truth does not depend on quantity of detail or mathematical accuracy but on the manipulation of all the stresses in a chosen style. This is why he was always emphasising the need to "work at values".

Corot's long experience before nature enabled him to effect a reconciliation of a kind between the sketch and the composed studio picture. In the last thirty years of his life there is in his work a slow drawing together of the threads. Straightforward views such as *The Road from Sèvres* (plate 37) or the panoramic vista of *Rouen* (plate 36) are more composed, for example, than the early Italian sketches. *The Belfry at Douai* (plate 45) has a weight and monumentality that is hard to equal in the youthful landscapes taken direct from nature.

In the big Salon pictures, such as the *Macbeth* of 1859 (plate 38), the handling becomes looser and the details less numerous. The laborious contrivance of the earlier "machines" gives way to a smooth, unified sense of mood that is akin to the single atmospheric condition that may dominate the natural scene at any given time. This feeling for mood, often called poetic for want of any more precise term, is something that the sentimental taste of the second half of the nineteenth century greatly appreciated. Hence the popularity of canvases like the *Souvenir de Mortefontaine* (plate 43).

The composition of these pictures is seldom of much interest. The figures are conventional and so are the props. The strongest element is the mood. And it is strong because it is the one element in the later Salon pictures about which Corot, a poor liar, really cared. It mattered to him because it was inseparably linked in his own mind with the harmonising of colours. He always remained, first and foremost, a *technician*. When he went to Italy for the first time, he learned that introduction of white lead into all the pigments produced not only accuracy but harmony. As the years went by, Corot came to realise that this harmony was the one truly positive thing that he could offer up at the altars of classical landscape painting. And as the 1840s merged into the 1850s this is what he began to impose on the classical framework. The *Souvenir of Castelgandolfo* (plate 44) belongs in the same tradition as the *Bridge at Narni* (plate 6) but the more unified effect, the merging of the forms and the blending of the colours now stamp it far more firmly with Corot's own private signature.

Claude was much concerned with evocation of mood but in his work it is always more specific and literary. He wished to re-create a lost world in which man had lived in complete accord with nature, the Golden Age celebrated in antique poetry. Corot leaned heavily on the Claudian tradition but the complex and subtle allusions escaped him. The harmony of Corot is neither religious nor philosophic. It is, as Oscar Wilde implies, musical.

Corot, was, in fact, very fond of music. All those who knew him emphasise how he loved to sing while he worked. When he was in Paris he attended concerts regularly. Beethoven, Gluck, Haydn, Mozart and Weber were his particular favourites. This feeling for music was linked in his own mind, instinctively rather than rationally, with his view of nature and his work. In front of an especially fine vista he was moved to exclaim: "What harmony! What grandeur! It is like Gluck." "I have only a little flute," he was fond of telling Pissarro, "but I try to strike the right note." The musical analogy is implicit in the comparison he drew between Delacroix and himself. If Delacroix was an eagle, Corot said, he was but a mere lark.

Harmony is, as we have seen, a key feature of the oil sketches. But in these, while strong, it is also non-committal. Corot knew that Salon painting was about something more positive. Larger issues were involved. It is possible that he realised, only half consciously but in a way sufficiently striking to influence his painting, that harmony in music fulfils a double function. It can construct something that is unified, while at the same time creating a directed response, an evocation of a mood or an emotion. And it is this specific combination of surface harmony and a sense of mood that is strong, but at the same time curiously elusive, that makes Corot's later work seem so musical in character.

But Corot was not an abstract artist and this creation of mood was inseparably linked to the observation of nature. He came to appreciate that the greatest coincidence between the natural effects that he could capture on canvas, and the strong pictorial mood that he wanted, lay in the phenomena of dawn and dusk. That is why so many of his later canvases reproduce the rising or the setting sun. These times of day had further charms for Corot. Though subtle in gradation — and his technique was perfectly suited to that — sunset and sunrise are also very *obvious* and this no doubt appealed to his simplicity of heart. They can also be melancholic; and Corot had a streak of melancholy in him. They also make a very direct attack on our sentiments.

In *Macbeth* (plate 38) or the *Souvenir de Mortefontaine* (plate 43) it is possible to sound the true depths of Corot's sentimentality. The pictures are sentimental. There is about them, as there was in Corot's own character, something virginal and pulpy, a quality of feeling that is pure and, in its measure, full, if not overflowing, but at the same time soft; without either the strength or the restraint that a wider acceptance of life and a more couragous contact with experience and ideas would have produced.

During the last half century these later paintings have had a poor response from critics. It is not hard to see why. The sketches are miraculous but silent. In the big Salon paintings the artist "speaks" in the pictorial sense of the word. The only trouble is that he does not seem to be saying anything we wish to hear. Who would now agree with Paul de Saint-Victor when he wrote, in 1855, that "we prefer the Sacred Grove peopled by fauns to the woodcutter's forest, and limpid springs where nymphs are bathing to Flemish ponds where ducks are paddling"? The feeling for colour harmonies is often profound but it is fatally attached to a kind of imagery that we neither value in a nineteenth-century context nor accept because the artist has made it his own. It is possible to lament that Corot, like a singer with a partiality for mediocre songs, should have wasted so much of his talent on such inferior material.

It is with some relief that we are able to turn to the monumental figure pieces that Corot began to produce in the 1850s. He had always painted figures, often, one may suppose, in the winter when the urge to record the object directly grew too strong to be satisfied with a mere reworking of his sketches.

In Italy, Corot had brought in old people, beggars and monks, etc., to sit for him (for example, plates 9, 10). Back in France, he concentrated on his family and friends (plates 33, 35). These are invariably straightforward little portraits, intimate, direct and unpretentious in spirit, and not unlike early daguerreotypes in character.

But in the last twenty years of his life Corot began to subject his figure pieces to the same kind of lyrical overtones he was introducing into his landscapes. *The Young Girls of Sparta* (plate 47) bears the same kind of relationship to *The Old Man Sitting on Corot's Trunk* (plate 9) as the *Souvenir de Castelgandolfo* (plate 44) does to one of the early Italian studies. Many of the figure pieces escape the weaknesses inherent in the contemporary landscape, through a mixture of stability and directness. Though he dressed them up, the models were still there in front of him. The recording process reasserts itself at the expense of poetry and sentimentality. And since the single figure is an easier element to compose than a whole landscape, Corot's instinctive feeling for classical composition is revealed to us, in *The Woman with a Pearl* (Louvre) or the superb *Femme en bleu* (plate 51) for example, in a more direct, less diluted form. The best of these later figure pieces fully justify Degas' famous reply to a friend who once asked him if he thought Corot could draw a tree properly: "I am going to surprise you," Degas remarked, "he draws a figure even better."

Corot tried exhibiting these figure pieces but they did not please. Only two were ever publicly shown. The now famous sketches from nature were almost as hidden from the public gaze. It was not until the Jury of the Salon was suppressed in 1848, and the choice of exhibits widened, that Corot had dared to show one of his Italian sketches (*The Colosseum* of 1826, now in the Louvre) in public. With the swing in taste, the figure pieces and the sketches are what are now valued most. Because they were "hidden away" we are too easily inclined to assume that they were the revolutionary works of a revolutionary talent. This would be a subtle distortion. To the extent that they were not what the public wanted, and to the extent that the sketches anticipate the Impressionists, the pictures are revolutionary. As far as Corot himself was concerned, however, any qualities that we are inclined to think of now as revolutionary were, like coke, merely the by-product of a process; he adored working out of doors. The famous *Belfry at Douai* (plate 45) was painted in 1874 and has often been compared to an Impressionist landscape. But Corot himself would not have cared for the comparison.

He hated factions. And he would not take sides. When an old pupil, Antoine Guillemet (1841-1918) refused to join the Impressionists Corot congratulated him: "You were damned right to get out, my boy." And when Daubigny tried to enlist his support for the young painters, at the time of the reorganisation of the Salon in 1870, Corot wriggled out of the responsibilities. Just as he liked his many kindnesses to those in need to be as surreptitious as possible, so he wanted his fame and his work to exist without strings. Factions were both an irrelevance and a distraction. He did not see art in intellectual terms. And he knew he was old-fashioned. After seeing Millet's *Gleaners* (Louvre) at the Salon of 1857, he had written: "It is a new world. I don't see myself in it. I am too attached to the old ways." He "saw silver and blond" when everyone else was "seeing green".

But Corot also knew that he was famous. At the beginning of the 1850s he already had a string of pupils, including, from 1855, the young Pissarro; and there were already imitators. He had been on the Jury of the Salon in 1849 and again in 1851. In 1855 he had been awarded a first class medal at the World Fair in Paris. And Napoleon III had purchased *La Charette: Souvenir de Marcoussis* (Louvre). This single act, more than any other, had broken down the last barriers of formal opposition. There had been from that moment on an enormous demand for Corot's work; and in the 1860s American clients had added their voice to the general clamour. And when he had sent 28 paintings to a sale in 1858 Corot had been so amazed at the high prices that he suspected some trickery. So popular did he become that he was obliged to rent a "secret" studio in the Rue Fontaine where he might work undisturbed.

As the years went by Corot grew into the venerable, white-haired "Papa Corot". And this image glowed ever brighter as the news of his many acts of generosity spread. He assisted Hervier and Harpignies; he bought a house at Auvers for Daumier when he had grown old and blind; he went to the aid of Aligny's widow; and he gave ten thousand francs to help the destitute family of Millet. He gave constantly to the refuge for babies in the Rue Vandrezanne, where they hung his portrait in the dormitory. He would retouch and sign landscapes by needy students and he would only sell his own work to one particular dealer on condition that he also bought pictures by the struggling young Lépine. Corot was truly worth the epithet his contemporaries gave him. They called him "the St Vincent de Paul of painting."

Nothing can tarnish his kindness and generosity, which was as instinctive as it was fine. But it is worth recording that he did not care about money. He had always had enough to live on and the money he inherited (not to mention the income accruing from his pictures), made no difference to his way of life. His studios always revealed an almost spartan absence of luxury. He had no library to speak of and did not greatly care for reading. *The Imitation of Christ* by Thomas à Kempis is one of the few books he is known to have read with enthusiasm. "It is this book", he told Madame Aviat, when they were painting together at Méry sur Aube in 1871, "which has helped me to pass my life with so much calm and always leaves me with a happy heart."

He was not a collector like Degas. Other people's work did not greatly interest him. Corot's clothes were always of the simplest, almost crude, and his early background did not instil into him any sense of chic.

He had an instinctive eye for the shade of a tone in landscape and an equally instinctive feeling for harmonies of colour. This mingling of science and taste functioned from the very beginning. Its achievement depended on effort and hard work but it involved no real expansion of the intellect. The character of Corot's art altered and softened as he grew older but the change demanded no breaking out, no radical departures. He had been brought up in the classical tradition of landscape painting and did not have any inclination to relate it to modern life. This reactionary approach to his painting sealed him off from both the new realism of Courbet and from the equally novel form of naturalism practised by the Impressionists.

Dozens of contemporary academic painters remained sealed off as well. They have been forgotten. Many of them were far more intelligent than Corot. Fromentin, indeed, was a discerning critic and a novelist whose *Dominique* may still be read with pleasure and respect. But as a painter he is dead as mutton.

But it was not the opposite, mere innocence, that saved Corot. It was an innocence inseparable from a skill that did not, because it was so instinctive, impinge on his character. This kind of artist is more common in the visual and the performing arts than in literature. It is very hard to go on writing serious novels of quality for fifty years without broadening and deepening the personality, which, as it matures, has a corresponding effect on the work produced.

The innocence that runs so strongly through Corot's character showed itself in a variety of ways. It was in his goodness, the sheer kindness that made him seem to contemporaries "adorably good". It was the opposite of curiosity and experience and became a part of the complacency that Corot undoubtedly had. He liked his own pictures very much indeed, he kept them about him and he would buy them back years after they had been painted. Innocence was also a part of his acceptance of things. He had accepted his home life and the worn out traditions of classical landscape. He accepted society and the aesthetic standards of the day which are unconsciously reflected in his painting. So that the *Souvenir de Castelgandolfo* (plate 44) seems as symptomatic of the Second Empire as the Paris Opéra.

Corot also accepted the personal regime he had laid down for himself in his youth. He never suddenly decided that he was going to have a year off and do nothing but read or go to America. He worked and worked. And in his seventies he was still getting up at half past six in the morning, quite prepared to work on duckboards under an umbrella if it rained. And as the years went by, Corot began to accept what the world thought of him as an image to be presented. It is possible that his later Salon landscapes would not have been quite so nymph-ridden had critics not been telling him, since the beginning of the 1840s, just how lyrical and classical his works were.

In his old age he was "Papa Corot". He played up to the role. He knew quite well that everyone thought of him as a benevolent old man and since that is exactly what he was he saw no harm in raising, so to speak, the volume of the performance. Silvestre, who knew him well, once remarked that he thought Corot tended to exaggerate the gaiety of his character. And sometimes it does seem possible to detect, all but obliterated by the genial glow of his kind heart and great reputation, a fleeting image of sadness, perhaps no more than a melancholy smile, the occasional sigh of a man who has abstained from life not wisely but too well. A certain Mlle Rose had worked as a girl in his mother's shop in the 1820s. "She is still alive," said Corot in 1858, "and has never been married, and even now she occasionally pays me a visit. She was here only last week. Oh, my friends, what changes have taken place since then, and what reflections they give rise to!"

Some writers have tried to weave a romance round Corot and Mlle Rose. It is a charming notion but unfortunately it does not take into account the streak of sheer peasant obstinacy in Corot's make-up. Wives and mistresses, it is safe to say, he cut out of his life because they would have needed too much care and attention. Though he could be kind with his money, Corot was tight-fisted with his time. He was fond of staying with people, and would gladly accept invitations, but always on the tacit understanding that he could carry on working as usual.

Innocence, discipline and acceptance, then, are at the very core of his achievement as an artist. Few great artists have maintained themselves so well on such limited resources as Corot. For fifty years he painted landscapes out of doors and at the end of his life he was still producing works as fresh and beautiful as he had done at the beginning. The simplest answer would be to say — and say correctly — that his skill had not declined. But it is hard to believe that he could have kept up his level of achievement if his skill had not been constantly saturated with delight, if the sheer act of painting had not also been an act of unquestioning joy.

This is why he was always stressing the importance of emotion in work. "In nature", he once wrote, "look for form, then the values in relation to tone, colour and execution, the whole governed by the emotion you have experienced." This emotion was also deeply connected with the physical sensation of actually being in the country. "For six months", we find Corot writing in 1867, "I have laboriously worked on boughs in my studio. I need living boughs, I want to see how the leaves of the willow grow from their branches. I am going to the country. When in July I bury my nose in a hazel-bush, I shall be fifteen years old." When he wrote that he was seventy-one.

The Impressionists, too, painted landscapes out of doors, and they too greatly enjoyed their work, but after barely fifteen years they had run into serious trouble. By the early 1880s Renoir, Monet and Pissarro had all begun to realise that ensnaring an impression of a scene on canvas was no longer enough. What they mutually desired and what they sought to find, each after his own fashion, was a more intellectual basis for their art. Renoir experimented with strict drawing, Monet began to seize upon more and more *recherché* optical effects, while Pissarro sought to codify Impressionism in a form of pointillism.

Curiosity breeds change. But Corot was never curious and the secret of his continued and serene successes lies not only in a certain religious innocence but also in his continued acceptance of the impression produced on his eyes.

The *appearance* of buildings and trees at certain times of the day, under certain conditions of light, remained, so far as Corot was concerned, entirely valid subject matter for his skill. This act of faith produced one of the largest *oeuvres* in art.

It is an *œuvre* that is, as was suggested at the beginning, difficult to evaluate. Corot never got so much out of a landscape, when he was working in front of it, as did Cézanne, nor was he able through sheer invention to put as much into it as did Pieter Brueghel. But his skill and taste carried him far, so far in fact that it is possible to feel that the *View of Florence from the Boboli Gardens* (plate 18) is the most beautiful landscape produced in France in the nineteenth century. Even so, Corot cannot perhaps, in the final analysis, be placed among the very greatest masters of the genre. The absolute radiance of true imagination does not illuminate his work as it does that of Claude and Turner, Rubens and Brueghel. But the greater the attempt, the greater the contrivance. Great nails are being hit on the head; and the sheer, heroic force of the blows will echo through the works for ever. Corot, in the works that will truly last, belongs to a very rare group of artists who hit nails with an almost silent hammer. Such beauty, at the expense of so little effort, such accuracy, devoid of any trite, pointed direction, baffle at the same time as they satisfy the spectator. It is impossible to find just the right category for *La Trinité des Monts* (plate 4), *Monsieur Pivot on Horseback* (plate 33) or the *Femme en bleu* (plate 51). Their enigmatic and seamless beauty takes them out of a humble category without, at the same time, providing a wholly assured passport to larger frames of reference. Like a Mozart serenade or a nocturne by Chopin, they float free of criticism. They cannot be explained; only felt. Which is perhaps as it should be in the case of an artist who set such store by feeling.

OUTLINE BIOGRAPHY OF COROT

1796	Birth of Jean-Baptiste-Camille Corot in Paris on July 16th.
1803—1807	A boarder at M. Letellier's school in the Rue de Vaugirard, Paris.
1807—1812	At the Lycée in Rouen.
1812—1814	At a boarding school at Poissy.
1814—1821	Apprenticed to two cloth merchants.
1822	Finally allowed to take up painting. Corot's father gives him an allowance of 1500 francs. Studies with Michallon and Bertin.
1825—1828	In Italy. Travelling from spring to autumn and working out of doors. Works in the studio in winter. Sends back two pictures for the 1827 Salon.
1833	Awarded a second class medal at the Salon of 1833.
1834	Second trip to Italy, cut short by news of his father's illness.
1840	First acquisition of his work by the State: *Le Petit Berger* (shown at the Salon of 1840) bought for the Museum at Metz.
1842	Visit to Switzerland.
1843	Third and final trip to Italy.
1846	Awarded the Legion of Honour.
1847	Death of Corot's father.
1848	The *Site d'Italie* bought by the state for the Museum at Douai. Corot wins a second class medal at the Salon.
1849	A member of the Jury for the Salon. Exhibits, for the first time, a study after nature: the 1826 view of the Colosseum now in the Louvre. The

Christ au Jardins des Oliviers acquired by the State for the Museum at Langres.

1851 Death of Corot's mother. He is again on the Jury of the Salon.

1852 Shows, for the first time at the Salon, a study after nature made in France — *The Port of La Rochelle*. Comes into contact with Alfred Robaut, who was to be his biographer and the initial compiler of the monumental catalogue raisonné.

1853 Travels, with the painter Daubigny, to Geneva.

1854 Visits Holland in August and September.

1855 Awarded a first class medal at the World Fair in Paris. *La Charette: Souvenir de Marcoussis* bought by Napoleon III.

1862 Visits London for the International Exhibition. Paints three pictures in or around London.

1864 Member of the Jury for the Salon.

1867 Ill with gout. Awarded a second class medal at the World Exhibition. Promoted to Officer of the Legion of Honour.

1870 A member of the Jury for the Salon. Remains in Paris during the Franco-Prussian War, helping the needy.

1873 Builds a studio at Coubron.

1874 Death of his sister.

1875 Death of Corot on February 22nd.

NOTES ON THE PLATES

The references to "Robaut" in the Notes on the Plates are from A. Robaut *L'œuvre de Corot: Catalogue raisonné et illustré, précédé de l'histoire de Corot et de son œuvre par E. Moreau-Nélaton* 4 vols., Floury, Paris, 1905.

Plate 1 *Self-portrait at the Age of 29.* Canvas: 12⁵/₈ × 9¹/₈ in. (32 × 24 cm.). Louvre, Paris.
Painted in 1825 in accordance with M. Corot's wish that his son should leave behind a self-portrait when he went to Italy. Robaut no. 41.

Plate 2 *Le Petit Chaville, near Ville-d'Avray.* Canvas: 9¹/₈ × 13 in. (24 × 33 cm.). Ashmolean Museum, Oxford.
Painted about 1823-5. Repeated in a larger version in 1855. Bought back by the artist in 1874. Both this and the *Self-portrait* (plate 1) show how developed Corot's technique was even before he set foot in Italy. They are thickly painted and they reveal already a strong feeling for tonal harmony. Robaut no. 16.

Plate 3 *View of the Forum from the Farnese Gardens.* Canvas: 11 × 19¹¹/₁₆ (28 × 50 cm.). Left by Corot to the Louvre at his death in 1875.
Signed and dated March, 1826. Painted in fifteen afternoon sittings. Corot used this picture as the basis for several other, later, canvases, including a larger one (45 × 79 cm.) painted, about 1845, for his friend M. Robert of Mantes. The foreground is much more elaborate, after the manner of Claude. Robaut no. 67.

Plate 4 *La Trinité des Monts, Rome.* Canvas: 17¹¹/₁₆ × 29¹/₈ in. (45 × 74 cm.). Louvre, Paris.
Painted about 1826-8. Unfinished. The area to the right, with the Spanish Steps, is omitted. Note also how Corot avoids any kind of detailed treatment of the foreground. All the attention is focused on the buildings in the middle and far distance. Robaut no. 83.

Plate 5 *The Bridge at Narni.* Canvas: 13³/₈ × 18¹/₂ in. (34 × 47 cm.). Louvre, Paris.
Inscribed on the back: *Étude donnée par Corot à son ami Lapito.* A preliminary study for plate 6. Robaut no. 130.

Plate 6 *The Bridge at Narni.* Canvas: 26³/₈ × 36⁵/₈ in. (67 × 93 cm.). National Gallery of Canada, Ottawa (acquired 1940).
Painted in the studio, presumably in the winter of 1826-7. Sent to the Paris Salon of 1827 (no. 221). The picture was, apparently, hanging over Corot's bed at the time of his death and it was lot 21 in the sale of the studio contents.
The Bridge at Narni is a revealing example of the difference between the sketch from nature and the kind of elaborate, composed view with figures deemed suitable for public exhibition. Robaut no. 199.

Plate 7 *The Roman Campagna with the Claudian Aqueduct.* Canvas: 8¹/₄ × 13 in. (21 × 33 cm.). National Gallery, London. Painted about 1826/8.
The picture was bought at the Doria Sale in Paris (May, 1899) by Degas and it figured in his posthumous sale (March, 1918), whence it was purchased for the National Gallery. Robaut no. 98 bis.

Plate 8 *La Cervara — The Roman Campagna.* Canvas: 26³/₄ × 37³/₈ in. (68 × 95 cm.). Kunsthaus, Zürich.
Painted about 1825-8 and shown at the Paris Salon of 1831. A picture that suggests the influence on Corot of Gaspar Dughet. In spite of the overall artificiality, the details themselves are brilliantly handled. Note how the grey surface of the storm cloud is thinned down in places to the brown ground to suggest the warm sun pressing against the mist. Robaut no. 200.

Plate 9 *Old Man Sitting on Corot's Trunk.* Canvas: 13 × 9¹/₁₆ in. (32 × 23 cm.). Museum of Fine Arts, Boston.
Dated February, 1826. A good, early example of Corot's treatment of the figure, which he approached with the same detachment that he showed in front of landscape. Corot bought back this sketch in the early 1870s. Robaut no. 89.

Plate 10 *Italian Monk Seated, Reading.* Canvas: 15³/₄ × 10⁵/₈ in. (40 × 27 cm.). Albright-Knox Art Gallery, Buffalo, N.Y.
Painted about 1827. By this date, Corot's technique was subtler and more assured than it had been in France. The handling of the paint is thinner now, more delicate and less pasty. This is the kind of figure study that Corot, following Michallon's example, would paint in the studio.

He often depicted monks in contemplative poses that were not only apt for the sitter but also justified the stillness he liked all his subject matter to have. Robaut no. 105.

Plate 11 *Cathedral of Chartres.* Canvas: $25^3/_{16} \times 20^1/_{16}$ in. (64×51 cm.). Louvre, Paris.
Painted in 1830, when, at the outbreak of the July Revolution, Corot decided to leave Paris. In 1872, Corot slightly modified the picture, principally in the foreground. He added the man sitting on the big stone at the left and retouched the man smoking his pipe in the middle. Robaut no. 221.

Plate 12 *View of Soissons.* Canvas: $31^1/_2 \times 39^3/_8$ in. (80×100 cm.). Kröller-Müller Museum, Otterlo.
Signed and dated 1833. The view is from the house of a certain M. Henry, a manufacturer of furnishing fabrics, for whom Corot painted this and a pendant, showing his patron's house. Corot was not paid for the pictures and was satisfied to receive board and lodgings during the period of work. Note the elaborate and artificial foreground. Robaut no. 244.

Plate 13 *The Forest of Fontainebleau.* Canvas: $68^7/_8 \times 96^7/_{16}$ in. (175×245 cm.). National Gallery of Art, Washington (Chester Dale Collection).
Signed at the bottom right. The exact date of this elaborate and rather academic landscape is uncertain. *Une Forêt* appeared at the Salons of 1831 and 1834. Robaut no. 225. This is perhaps the painting referred to by Lenormant. (See page 23.)

Plate 14 *View of Genoa.* Canvas: $11^7/_{16} \times 16^1/_8$ in. (29×41 cm.). Art Institute, Chicago (Mr and Mrs Martin A. Ryerson Collection)
Painted in June, 1834. Robaut no. 301.

Plate 15 *View of the Quay of the Schiavoni, Venice.* Canvas: $12^1/_4 \times 17^{11}/_{16}$ in. (31.1×45 cm.). National Gallery of Victoria, Melbourne (Felton Bequest).
Probably a study after nature, made on the second visit to Italy in 1834. Corot painted a larger version in 1848 for his friend, M. Robert of Mantes (Robaut no. 322). Robaut no. 321.

Plate 16 *View of Volterra.* Canvas: $27^1/_2 \times 36^5/_8$ in. (70×93 cm.). Louvre, Paris.
Painted in 1834, on the second Italian visit. Robaut no. 303.

Plate 17 *Hagar in the Wilderness.* Canvas: $69^{11}/_{16} \times 105^1/_8$ in. (177×267 cm.). Metropolitan Museum of Art, New York (Rogers Fund, 1938).
An illustration to Genesis XXI, 17, 18. One of the most important of the big, "historical" landscapes by which Corot sought to make his name in the 1830s. The picture was begun before the second Italian trip of 1834 but he was unable to complete it satisfactorily. It was finished after the visit and sent to the Salon of 1835, where it gained much favourable attention. It remained, however, unsold and the artist kept it until his death. The "wilder-

ness of Beersheba" was based on studies made in the Sabine mountains near Narni and Terni. Robaut no. 362.

Plate 18 *Florence from the Boboli Gardens.* Canvas: $20^1/_{16} \times 29$ in. (51×73.5 cm.). Louvre, Paris (acquired 1926). This is a more developed version, dating from the second half of the 1830s, of a smaller sketch (Robaut no. 309) made in Florence between July and August, 1834. Robaut no. 310.

Plate 19 *View of Villeneuve-lès-Avignon.* Canvas: $15 \times 22^1/_{16}$ in. (38×56 cm.). Musée des Beaux-Arts, Reims.
Painted about 1836. A smaller variant is in the Mestag Museum at The Hague. A superb example of Corot's perfect control of tone.

Plate 20 *A View near Volterra.* Canvas: $25^3/_4 \times 37^3/_8$ in. (69.5×95 cm.). National Gallery of Art, Washington (Chester Dale Collection).
Signed and dated 1838. Either this, or a similar though narrower picture, was exhibited at the Salon of 1838, where it met with a cool reception.

Plate 21 *Ville d'Avray: les maisons Cabassud.* Canvas: $10^5/_8 \times 15^3/_8$ in. (27×39 cm.). Louvre, Paris.
Painted about 1835-40. This view, which Corot painted several times, is from the Corot family property. Robaut no. 284.

Plate 22 *The Banks of the Cousin.* (Morvan Hills). Canvas: $14^3/_{16} \times 11^7/_{16}$ in. (36×29 cm.). Louvre, Paris (Personnaz Bequest, 1935).
Painted about 1840-45. A fine example of Corot's more intimate nature studies. But even here the focus is in the distance; and the foreground receives summary treatment Robaut no. 430.

Plate 23 *Saint-André-en-Morvan.* (Nièvre). Canvas: $12^3/_{16} \times 23^1/_4$ in. (31×59 cm.). Louvre, Paris.
Signed and dated 1842. After having been lost, the picture was recovered by Corot in 1872. Corot frequently worked in the Morvan region, where one of his nieces, Madame Baudot, lived. Robaut no. 424.

Plate 24 *View of the Château de Pierrefonds.* (Oise). Canvas: $19^5/_{16} \times 30^{11}/_{16}$ in. (49×78 cm). Musée de Quimper.
Signed. Painted about 1840-45. This picture shows Corot's continued partiality for a solid, dominating "motif" in the distance as the focal centre of a painting. Robaut, no. 474.

Plate 25 *La Marietta.* Canvas: $11^7/_{16} \times 28^9/_{16}$ in. (29×42 cm.). Musée du Petit Palais, Paris.
Inscribed at the top left: *Marietta à Rome.* Painted in 1843 on the third and final visit to Italy. The influence of Ingres is apparent in the composition. The single nude figure, treated as a study, is rare in Corot's work. Robaut no. 458.

Plate 26 *View of the Church of St Paterne at Orleans.* Canvas: $11 \times 27^3/_4$ in. (28×40 cm.). Musée des Beaux-

Arts, Strasbourg.

Painted about 1840-45. Corot often painted a scene, as in this case, from the upper floor of a building: no doubt in order to avoid the crowds of curious onlookers who would cluster round his easel had he set it down in the street. A signed replica of this picture was in the Doria Sale, May, 1899 (lot 70). Robaut no. 555.

Plate 27 *View of Naples*. Canvas: $26^3/_4 \times 42^1/_2$ in. (68 × 108 cm.). Museum of Fine Arts, Springfield.
Signed and dated 1841. Shown at the Salon of 1841 (398). Given by the artist to M. Robert of Mantes. A clear example of Claudian influence. The plants in the foreground, the framing trees on the right, the subsidiary vista to the left, the distant sea and mountains are all used in a similar way to the works of Claude. The colouring is softer and more fused now and lends support to Baudelaire's dictum that "M. Corot is a harmonist rather than a colourist". Robaut no. 377.

Plate 28 *Homer and the Shepherds*. Canvas: $31^1/_2 \times 51^3/_{16}$ in. (80 × 130 cm.). Musée de Saint-Lô.
For the landscape background, Corot made use of a study made at Royat in 1839. The picture was shown at the Salon of 1845 (364). Baudelaire, in his account of the exhibition, wrote enthusiastically about *Homer and the Shepherds*: "there is nothing unnecessary, nothing to be pruned — not even the two little figures walking away in conversation down the path. The three little shepherds with their dog are enchanting, like those excellent little scraps of bas-relief which are sometimes to be found on the pedestals of antique statues." Robaut no. 464.

Plate 29 *The Forest of Fontainebleau*. Canvas: $35^7/_{16} \times 51^3/_{16}$ in. (90 × 130 cm.). Museum of Fine Arts, Boston.
Shown at the Salon of 1846, the year in which Corot was awarded the Legion of Honour. The composition was based on a study made in the forest (in the Gorges d'Apremont) in 1834. In the larger and later picture, however, the rocks and earthworks in the foreground have been replaced by the pond. The painting was noted, favourably, by Baudelaire in his account of the 1846 Salon. Robaut no. 502.

Plate 30 *La Danse des Nymphes*. Canvas: $38^3/_{16} \times 51^3/_{16}$ in. (97 × 130 cm.). Louvre, Paris.
Shown at the Salon of 1850-51 (643), where it was bought by the State for 1500 francs. It entered the Luxembourg in 1855 and the Louvre in 1887. One of the most Claudian of all Corot's pictures. The silvery blues and greyish greens are symptomatic of the softer and more fused colour scale the artist was evolving in the 1840s. Although the big clump of trees to the right is of a kind favoured by Claude, it was actually taken, directly, from a study that Corot had made in the Farnese Gardens in Rome (1826-8. Robaut no. 54). Robaut no. 1061.

Plate 31 *The Port of Rochelle*. Canvas: $31^{11}/_{16} \times 27^{15}/_{16}$ in. (50 × 71 cm.). Yale University Art Gallery (Bequest of Stephen Carlton Clark).
Painted, in 1851, from the window of a house on the

Quai Valin. This is the first direct nature study made in France that Corot exhibited at the Salon (1852, no. 283). The canvas was much exhibited in Corot's lifetime: Rouen, 1856, Toulouse, 1865, Amiens and Arras, 1868, etc. Robaut no. 669.

Plate 32 *Breton Women at the Well*. Canvas: $14^{15}/_{16} \times 21^5/_8$ in. (38 × 55 cm.). Louvre, Paris.
Painted, in the first half of the 1850s, in the neighbourhood of Croisic. One of the rare studies from nature in which figures play a prominent part. Robaut no. 684.

Plate 33 *Monsieur Pivot on Horseback*. Canvas: $15^3/_8 \times 11^3/_4$ in. (39 × 30 cm.). National Gallery, London.
Painted in the first half of the 1850s, this is the only equestrian portrait Corot ever made. M. Pivot was a neighbour of the artist at Ville d'Avray. One day when Corot was working out of doors, he rode by. The painter was struck by the group against the woodland setting, and he asked M. Pivot if he would mind pausing while he made a study. The picture was borrowed from M. Pivot's widow so that Robaut might examine it in connection with his proposed catalogue. By mistake, it was included in the catalogue of the studio sale (no. 358) but was withdrawn. Robaut no. 665.

Plate 34 *Portrait of Mme Bison*. Canvas: $12^5/_8 \times 9^{13}/_{16}$ in. (32 × 25 cm.). Ashmolean Museum, Oxford.
Painted in 1852. A companion portrait of the lady's husband, who was a well-to-do Parisian merchant, is also in the Ashmolean. In small portraits of this kind, Corot was perhaps influenced by the daguerreotype. Robaut no. 1056.

Plate 35 *Portrait of Maurice Robert*. Canvas: $11^7/_{16} \times 9^1/_{16}$ in. (29 × 23 cm.). Louvre, Paris.
Painted at Mantes on April 12th, 1857. Maurice Robert was one of the children of Louis Robert, a magistrate of Mantes with whom Corot had enjoyed a warm friendship since 1840. One of the latest, as well as being one of the most beautiful of Corot's straightforward portraits. Robaut no. 1052.

Plate 36 *View of Rouen*. Canvas: $15^3/_4 \times 27^{15}/_{16}$ in. (40 × 71 cm.). Private Collection, Surrey.
Painted in the decade 1850-60. A direct study from nature. The trees, which were added afterwards, were probably introduced to give the final picture more of the air of a composed painting. Robaut no. 993.

Plate 37 *The Road from Sèvres, looking towards Paris*. Canvas: $13^3/_8 \times 18^7/_8$ in. (34 × 48 cm.). Louvre, Paris.
Painted about 1855-65. Corot produced two variants of this picture (Robaut, nos. 1463 and 1465). Robaut no. 1464.

Plate 38 *Macbeth and the Witches*. Canvas: $42^{15}/_{16} \times 53^1/_8$ in. (109 × 135 cm.). Wallace Collection, London.
Shown at the Salon of 1859. In later life Corot often drew inspiration from the theatre, to which he was devoted. In the original sketch for the picture (Robaut,

no. 1212), Macbeth is alone and on foot. Robaut no. 1109.

Plate 39 *Entrée de Village.* (In the neighbourhood of Beauvais). Canvas: $15^3/_4 \times 11^{13}/_{16}$ in. (40×30 cm.). Louvre, Paris.
Painted about 1855-65. This is the kind of unpretentious view of nature that would have influenced the Impressionists. The picture was brought to Corot, on the 1st of January, 1874, by the owner, so that it might be signed. Robaut no. 1003.

Plate 40 *La Danse des Bergères.* Canvas: $24^7/_{16} \times 31^1/_2$ in. (62×80 cm.). Louvre, Paris.
Painted in 1871. A study from nature, made at Arleux, and worked over in the studio. Robaut no. 2031.

Plate 41 *Young Girl at her Toilette.* Card: $13^3/_8 \times 9^7/_{16}$ in. (34×24 cm.). Louvre, Paris.
Painted in the first half of the 1860s. One of the most direct and unelaborated of Corot's later figure pieces. Robaut no. 1346.

Plate 42 *The Studio.* Canvas: $24^{13}/_{16} \times 16^9/_{16}$ in. (63×42 cm.). Louvre, Paris.
Painted about 1865-8. The later pictures of models in the studio suggest the influence of seventeenth-century Dutch genre painting; Corot is known to have admired Terboch. The studio represented is that in the Rue Paradis-Poissonière, where the artist worked during the last fifteen years of his life. Robaut no. 11559.

Plate 43 *Souvenir de Mortefontaine.* Canvas: $25^9/_{16} \times 33^1/_{16}$ in. (65×89 cm.). Shown at the Salon of 1864 (no. 442), where it was acquired by the State and placed in the Palace of Fontainebleau. In the Louvre since 1889. Repeated in varying formats, in the second half of the 1860s (Robaut nos. 1669-72). The most famous and, in many ways, the best of Corot's later studio landscapes. Although the scene is overlaid with sentimental adjuncts, the response to nature is still fresh and direct. The central feature of the picture, the reflection of the trees in the water, is surprisingly close to a Monet of the 1890s, such as the *Seine at Port-Villez* of 1894 in the Tate Gallery, London. Robaut no. 1625.

Plate 44 *Souvenir de Castelgandolfo.* Canvas: $25^9/_{16} \times 31^7/_8$ in. (65×81 cm.). Louvre, Paris.
Painted about 1865-8. A classic example of the later studio type of Corot, with its fused colour harmonies and strong, though rather undefined poetic mood. This picture should be compared with the earlier studio works (such as plates 6 and 8) Robaut no. 1626.

Plate 45 *The Belfry at Douai.* Canvas: $18^1/_2 \times 15^1/_8$ in. (46.5×38.5 cm.). Louvre, Paris.
Painted in 1871, from a window of a house on the angle of the Rue du Pont-à-l'herbe and the Rue de la Cloris. The picture was completed in twenty afternoon sessions, from 2 to 6 p.m. On May 8th, Corot wrote to Charles Desavary, then at Arras: "I am putting the last touches to the Beffroi de Douai, a splendid work . . ." Robaut no. 2004.

Plate 46 *The Gust of Wind.* Canvas: $18^1/_8 \times 20^{13}/_{16}$ in. (46×58 cm.). Musée des Beaux-Arts, Reims.
Painted in the second half of the 1860s. One of Corot's rare portrayals of nature in movement. Robaut no. 1906.

Plate 47 *The Young Girls of Sparta:* $16^9/_{16} \times 29^1/_2$ in. (42×75 cm.). Brooklyn Museum, New York.
Painted about 1868-70. The exoticism of Corot's later figure pieces, like this one, suggests the influence of Delacroix, whose work may also have prompted Corot to introduce single, strong notes of colour in a bodice or skirt. Robaut no. 1575.

Plate 48 *Mlle de Foudras.* Canvas: $34^3/_4 \times 20^1/_2$ in. (87.5×58.5 cm.). Glasgow Art Gallery.
Painted in 1872. The sitter was the daughter of a tobacconist living near Corot's Paris studio. A certain Leonardo-esque flavour in the shadowed modelling of the head is not, perhaps, entirely fortuitous. Corot certainly knew Da Vinci's work; *Woman with a Pearl* (Louvre; about 1868-70) deliberately echoes the pose of the *Mona Lisa*. Robaut no. 2133.

Plate 49 *The Tanneries at Mantes.* Canvas: $24 \times 16^9/_{16}$ in. (61×42 cm.). Louvre, Paris.
Painted on the spot in September, 1873. Corot was fond of telling friends how his work had been impeded by the appalling smells, the swarms of flies and the distractions of curious spectators. Robaut no. 2177.

Plate 50 *The Cart — Souvenir de Saintry.* Canvas: $18^1/_2 \times 20^1/_{16}$ in. (47×56 cm.). National Gallery, London.
Signed and dated 1874. A fine example of how fresh Corot's work remained right up to his death. Robaut no. 1976.

Plate 51 *La Femme en Bleu* Canvas: $31^1/_2 \times 19^{11}/_{16}$ in. (80×50.5 cm.). Louvre, Paris.
Signed and dated 1874. One of the finest of Corot's figure pieces. As usual, the painting has no strict meaning. But the superb control of the colour harmonies makes this hard to believe. Robaut no. 2180.

I

3

4

6

8

Janvier 1826   COROT

9

10

12

13

14

15

16

17

18

19

23

24

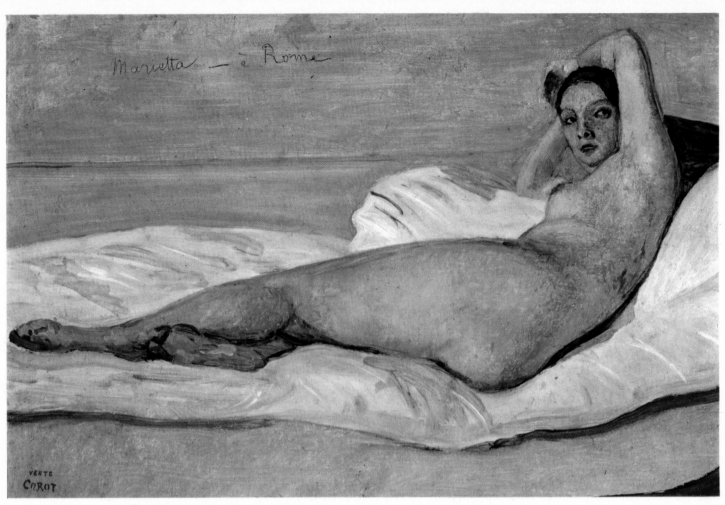

25

26

27

28

29

31

36

37

38

40

43

44

46

47

49